"ven aquí, corazón."

\-   *Jose Elmer Salgado*

Corazón

Yesika Salgado

Salgado, Yesika

ISBN: 978-1-945649-13-4

Edited by Safia Elhillo
Cover design by Cassidy Trier
Editorial design by Ian DeLucca

Not a Cult
Los Angeles, CA

Para
Mami y Papi
Jenny y Julie
Saya y Henry

Contents

The Return

when I first began piecing this book together I did not know if it would make sense. if I could turn my hunger for love, my poor choice in lovers, my impulsive destruction, my mouthful of tears into something tangible. I asked the poems what they wanted of me and I could hardly hear their whispers. then life happened. my heart was broken again. a relationship failed again. I had to dig myself out of the pain, again. I asked myself *how many times have I done this?* and I realized I had lost count. I am a woman who insists on loving love, who always finds a way back to herself, back to being whole. this book is for anyone who is all heart and not much else. if you fall easy. if you lose hard. if you are stubborn with your love. this is a celebration of the turns that love takes. the good. the confusing. the bad. the beauty of knowing we can always do it again. I hope you see yourself in my story, I hope you join me in celebrating our incredibly messy yet resilient hearts.

yours,
Yesika

The Hunger

Jenny and I

mangoes / the green ones / we used stones or large sticks
to knock from their branches / we'd sit and eat / then
and there / our small buckets in our laps / a bag of salt
between us / the cows and their large soft eyes would
stare / eyes like a first time lover / like a face so tender
it might cry / we were children then / you and I / our
grandmother Mamita was still alive / she stood at the
top of the hill and yelled our names / there was a river
behind us / a small quiet thing we'd wade into / when no
one was watching / one time you and the boys knocked
over a beehive / and ran so far up the hill it looked like
you were flying / I wasn't with you that day / I was afraid
of everything / except the poems / they've always been
here / you would leave for adventures in that country
we considered wild / all that green / all those animals / I
preferred my pen and paper / my bare feet on concrete
/ my hot coffee at 3 pm / overhearing Tia gossip with
Mamita / the green mangoes in their buckets / slowly
changing / like you and I / the summers I wore my
adolescence like a yoke / my heart as heavy as clay / love
a dangling fruit I ached to eat / and you remained a little
girl / laughing into a sky we call home / but know nothing
of

A Salvadoran Heart

I.
I come from women of corn and cotton fields / of machete
and fire / of water and stone / I am the daughter of a river
and mango tree / my tongue came to me through the
jocote seed / my heart belonged to the ocean / before it
found my body

II.
every man I have loved does not know my country / has
not been awakened by the roosters' crow / does not know
the swell of grass and dirt beneath June thunderstorms /
does not smell burning wood and think of home

III.
I learned to forgive before I learned to speak / to turn
palms upward to God and my lover / to let a man ruin
me with his love / to call the ruins sacred / to uproot
everything and call the new place mine / to name the
nostalgia something sweet / a ripened fruit growing out of
a dying tree

IV.
my father died and my mother remained alone / I am and
unmarried / I am asked if I want a husband / asked if I
will return to my country / they are the same question / I
do not want to answer

Cafe Con Pan

Papi would sit on the floor
his cafe con leche
poured into a bowl
he'd call me to him
placing strips of pan dulce
on a plate between us
together we'd drown them
into the coffee

from another room
Mami would say
deja de darle cafe a la niña
he'd laugh
kissing
the little rolls
on my legs

years later
when the alcohol
had done its work
and he was dying
I'd sit next to his bed
watching his shaking hands
dunk cookies into coffee

this is what I know of love

the sweet mouthful

a messy thing
dissolving
in my hands
on my tongue

filling everything

What I Know

1. all the bus routes that take you in and out of Downtown Los Angeles
2. the names of every street between Silverlake and Echo Park
3. what each store was before the gentrification
4. the corner we found my father on after a diabetic shock
5. the alley Mami had us walk through the night Papi hit her
6. the clinic where I saw my first therapist when I was 12
7. the parking lot where a drunk Papi tried to teach me to drive
8. the Rite Aid I got banned from for shoplifting
9. the store that doesn't I.D. for beer
10. the old Zoo
11. Griffith Park and its secret corners
12. Glendale and its shopping mall
13. Santa Monica beach and my two sisters
14. Papi's old car parked on our block
15. my body a glowing star within it
16. my first love and his hands around me
17. the jacaranda tree where I cried him out of me
18. the dead end where I took my next lover
19. the condom wrappers by the 101
20. Fairfax and Melrose

21. another lover and his car
22. his hand on my knee down Sunset
23. the apartment in Culver City
24. the break up in Westwood
25. in Hollywood
26. on Broadway
27. the hospital in East L.A.
28. the two fetuses it kept
29. California Hospital
30. my father, it kept
31. the grief I left everywhere
32. what this city takes
33. what this city gives
34. what I cannot forget
35. who I was before I knew
what I know now
before these
palm trees
loved me
back

Asking

I want love so bad
I chew on it in my sleep,
brush it into my gums

have you seen my quick smile?
this question laid across my face
asking
is it you? is it finally here?

I say I want love
but I know it's not true
when it comes,
what will I do
with this habit
of asking for what
I do not know how to keep?

Unknown

couples make me uncomfortable
how their bodies lean into each other
faces lit with the mischief of being publicly in love
one bold hand fitting into another
right there, where we all can see
I know love,
I learned it somewhere else
with no sun
and the windows shut
I am comfortable there

I think

Fat Girl Wants Love

I am in love / I am a fat girl / sometimes they are not the same thing / sometimes they are / he tells me he loves me / he keeps me a secret / I love him / I am a fat girl / this is the same this time / he doesn't have a name / he has too many names / I am good at loving in dark places / see: his mouth / see: his bedroom / see: the way I still smile when he lets my hand go in public / I love hungry / remember the time I ate my heart out in a movie theater / I was alone / remember the time I threw up all my fast food in a shopping mall bathroom / I was alone / remember the time I shoved my fingers down my throat / remember I failed / remember I wanted to die / remember when he kissed another woman in front of me / how I looked at her body / how I wanted her too / wanted to wear her / squeeze into her / I am a fat girl / I am in love / there is a joke here / he calls / my body wants to answer / my uncles used to say they needed longer arms to hug me / they would laugh / I would too / I grew up thinking no one could hold me / but he did / when no one was watching / it's okay / I don't watch myself all the time either / I am in love / I am hungry / this is synonymous / I wonder if my stomach and heart live in the same place / I gained weight again / I cry during my lunch break at work / I eat ice cream on my way home / I haven't been touched in months / someone rubs my back at an open mic and I feel the tears coming / I am a sad girl / I am a fat girl / I try and separate the two / I laugh a lot / I wear bright colors / things that say watch me / say come here / say wear me like a ribbon / a feather in your hat / something sweet on your lips / I want to believe it / I choose to believe it / I am in love / I forget with who / I say myself / most of the time it's true

Moonlighting

my girl broke up with her man months ago / yet here they
are / grinding on the dance floor / he / a salivating mouth
/ she / ripe fruit / I am not a person here / I am the disco
ball reflecting all over her face and his hands and her
thighs and his hips and their complicit smiles / wondering
what love like this tastes like / all I am is mirrors / another
name for this is poet / I write about love so much it fills a
room / but it ain't mine / I am good at reflecting / you can
also call this the moon / the couples are dancing beneath
my strobes / I drink another drink / hoping to consume
enough light / to climb out of my skin / and down to
dance

Cumbia

play a cumbia for me / que sea la sonora dinamita / that
one about no one knowing her suffering / play it / let me
dance to her broken heart / I am good at this / turning
heartache into a party / I learned it from my family / from
Papi and my Tios / I know there is no pain / some liquor
can't keep at bay / I also know the danger of that magic /
I play with it the way some play with fire / I was taught /
that death and power / are always served in the same cup

Celibacy

2 a.m.
there is a bed,
a body,
too many degrees,
sheets that stick to skin,
a mouth
with not
much to do
curls
around the night
the way
it could curl
around your salt
but
the body
is alone
in a bed
that feels
like stone
the body,
asleep now,
tosses one arm
over her head.
her mouth
empty.
what a shame.

After Another Bad Date

it isn't that I like him / it's that I like the idea of being
wanted / someone willing to open my doors and windows
/ let some light in where it hasn't been in a while / my
girl says he is wack and I can do better / I laugh / we are
at a bar and both our shoulders catch the neon lights /
we drink the night away despite our early mornings / this
is what I want / someone to lean into me with laughter
/ tonight it's her / tomorrow / ask me his name / I won't
remember / but my friend / her smile / I'll keep.

Friday Night

where do you want to meet?
the stranger asks via text

I, on the other side of the screen, smile coyly

anywhere
I type

in my head
a poem begins

this habit of
turning every man
into the next

15

Blind Date

what are your poems about?

I take my time stirring my coffee. I put a forkful of guava
cake in my mouth. I sip. I think of my parents, their
country, my sisters, my dead father, my dead grandmother,
my little niece and nephew, their perfect smiles, the men
I've loved to gluttony, the sex in the back seats of cars
and alleyways, the dance floors with a strange mouth to
my neck, my mother's graying hair, my overdrafted bank
account, my coffee-stained teeth, the times I've laughed
so hard the room spun, the moon at 3 a.m., I think of it all
and reach for the sugar. I spoon it into my cup.

mostly about me.

My Depression Has Questions

and if he loves you, what is next?
will you warn him about all your crying?
        it happens too often to ignore
        he will be telling you something
        about a coworker and suddenly
        there it is

the river behind your grandmother's house
winding down your face, your throat, your lap

are you going to ask if he can swim?

or will you wait,
hoping he drowns
like the rest?

Ansiedad

esta locura viene
y yo

pues

yo me voy con ella

Motherhood

I want to be a grandmother one day
but for this, I must be a mother first
though my body does not want motherhood
it tells the babies to go home
I am not a home

when the first baby bled out of me
my ex said it was okay
said he didn't want any children

the second baby I wanted to keep
the father did too
but when the blood bloomed
like a carnation
on my nightgown
my lover disappeared

now,
I have turned men into my children
I raise them
into who they never knew they could be
love them through their mistakes
reproach them when they stray too far
their lover and their mother
a hungry womb with no teeth
at night,
I hold their heads to my breasts
and breathe in their scent
aren't I a home baby?
and like this, we fall asleep

The Fruit

If you love me, even a little, I will call you corazón

Hand Holding

mine were warm
and yours were big enough
to lose mine in

I remember thinking
they were softer than I expected

my fingers slid between yours
- perfect
I said
you squeezed back a yes

we walked half a block like this
regular conversation
I don't know how
because all I was,
was a hand
being held by you

look at the moon,
you said

we stood
my body a kite
in the wind,
kissing the stars,
tethered
to land

to
you

Faith

I am not a religious woman
but I remember
the first time
I made you laugh

all the air around me
became a gown
the white of your teeth
something to walk
down an aisle for

I needed to find your God
and ask him to forgive me
for trying to love
anyone else
before you

A Kiss

I was drunk and he wasn't. we kissed and halfway
through, I laughed. my open mouth pressed over his open
mouth. he held me closer. laughed too. we shook with our
arms around each other. the sky wasn't a sky anymore.
it was the ground. I stopped being myself and he wasn't
my darling. instead, we were new. better than a moon. or
star. or sun. we were everything and nothing. we stood
that way for years or maybe seconds. laughing and kissing.
I don't remember what was funny. I only recall the
explosion. how in that moment I understood why I have
been willing to ruin myself for love. when it's good, it feels
like dying and being born all at once.

Aguacate

he scooped
the kiss out of me
as if I were
a ripened
avocado
sliced in half
and he
the spoon
come to
claim me

Communion

I want your mouth
between
my folds of skin
here, within the rolls
the part that is
a timid brown
the flesh that
doesn't know the sun
I want your kiss
in the places
only I have been
take my fat
and call it glory
call it supper
call it a meal
you'd ask for
on your knees
take this
bread
it is my body
now turned
yours

Overnight

I left my toothbrush
on his sink
in his bathroom
in his home

a tiny anchor
lowered into his port

stay here,
he said

and I did

Peluda

I used to leave your house before we fell asleep / tell you
I had to get home before work the next morning / explain
that I needed my own bed and hair products / you'd move
closer to me / lay an arm over my chest / *stay* / I would
blink at the ceiling / wait until your breathing grew heavy
/ slide out of bed and into my clothes / order an uber

the night sprawled out before me as I made my way home
/ to the razor blade in my shower / the hair on my chin
growing / a hundred little fingers ready to give me away /
ready to show you I am not the woman you think I am /
that sometimes I am grizzly / manic / human

one day / I didn't leave / you said love / I believed it /
the sun found me and my bearded chin in your kitchen
/ stirring oatmeal / your hands on my waist / a soft song
playing / *so this is what it means to stay*

Mine

let me / leave / lipstick prints on all your coffee mugs
a hair tie by the sink / socks in your blankets
take up space / mark you mine

Dulzura

mi corazón, cielito lindo, tesoro mío, mi amor, mi vida,
mi alma. — how beautiful it is to be loved in Spanish.
so much color. so much taste. this is where I learned to
love with abandon. when my lover called me his heart,
his pretty sky, his treasure, his love, his life, his soul —
has anyone ever spoken to you this way? covered you
with kisses naming you every precious thing they know?
have they filled you with so much dulce you thought you
would burst? — mi vida. mi alma. oh, to love so much you
become the soul, skies, treasure, corazón.

Mangos

it's too hot for clothes
we laugh, in our underwear
I slice two mangos for us
you stretch your legs out on the couch
baby, I say, handing you a fruit
you make room for me beside you
we spend the afternoon there

mouths
hands

sticky
sweet

Good Love

what about the happy love? all that good love that tells
you it's okay to stay in the house and watch Martin reruns
and you're not wondering where anyone else is because
all you ever wanted is there in that room on that couch
with you. what about the times you felt so much you
snuck into the kitchen to cry a little because everything
felt so good and you didn't know it was possible? you
didn't know you could love like that. love someone the
way your Mami loves. love someone and have them love
you right back. like that. like someone snapped their
fingers and gave you all the gold in the world. like you've
always been deserving of it and more. like you hadn't
been begging for scraps before. like you don't know how
to be loved any other way than this good way now. this
love that's got you glowing. this new name that you say
over and over. that's got you running around smiling at
strangers. looking at the world like it's an answer. like
the days are all working away at something. getting you
somewhere. someone. your lover. write about that. forget
the after. the part where it ends. or when it got quiet. that
doesn't matter right now. right here. what about the happy
love? it happened every time. every new love. remember?
remember?

The
Bruising

tell me you'll stay
and I'll stop pretending to leave

With And Without You

you love someone for a long time
so long you don't remember not loving them
so long the years accordion into each other
and within the folds, all the times you didn't get it right
so you let them go
they come back
(or you call them back)
you swear it'll be different
but it isn't
you still love them
each failure hurts
you think, maybe you can be friends
but that too is a sharp pain
you don't want them in your life
you don't want to live without them
another year goes by this way
turning hope into your only bread and water
maybe you'll figure it out
maybe someone new
will make you both
forget
maybe the world will end
and set you free

Familiar

come here
you call from the living room
I pull the chicken out of the oven
rip off a piece of its golden skin
walk barefoot across the tile, then carpet

baby, taste this
I hold it to your lips
you eat from my hands
pull me onto the couch

let's watch a movie
you click through the channels
land on Ace Ventura. I cringe

I hate Ace Ventura
I get up, serve us dinner
you eat yours on the couch
laughing loudly, smacking your lips
I have mine alone in the darkened dining room
the kitchen light casting shadows over my plate

baby, bring me more lemonade please

and finally, I am my mother's daughter

Molcajete

boil the tomatillos
boil the chiles
place them in the molcajete
with peeled garlic cloves

take the stone in your right hand
press it into the green
feel the tomatoes turn themselves inside out
the seeds of the chiles crawl out of their skin
the garlic become dozens of scattered teeth

lean in to the molcajete
as if waiting for a kiss
turn your hand as you grind the stone against stone
again, again, again

my mother would make the salsa verde for my father.
serve it to him during dinner. as if to say *here, this is what
my heart looks like*. he would spoon it into his tortilla. a
taco full of her. eyes watering between bites.

when you loved me I didn't know if I was the stone or the
hand
the tomatillos or the garlic

you were definitely the chile
you were the bite and the fire
you were the tears and tortilla

I sat my heart before you. watched you eat. waited for you
to tell me it tasted like home. you didn't.

Sacramento Airport

my driver picks me up at the Sacramento airport and we
head into Davis. he tells me it's been raining for days. he
points out the rice fields flooded with water. I am in the
backseat with hardly any words. I think of all that water,
how easily it can swell and swallow me. I wonder if it's
something I want. to be wiped clean. I'm thinking of you
again. your name exhausts me. I wonder if it stopped
being love and became a hunger. the driver asks if I am
married and I say yes. I like making new lives for myself
with strangers. today I am married to you and we don't
want children. I travel too much and you're getting your
degree. I imagine you in a small home somewhere in
Orange County, waiting for me. it's almost believable.
we pull up to my hotel. I am me again. consumed by
belonging to you. what an illness.

The Hennessy Calls Him

what are we?
do you still love me?
have you moved on?
what are we?
why can't I forget you?
why can't I forget?
do you still love me?
what are we doing?
what are we?
how do I stop being a question?
how do I become myself again?

A Seed, Your Name

I ate a mango in bed tonight
it is not mango season
but there it was
sitting in the produce section
slowly ripening
asking me a question
I've been asking myself
all week
is this really what I want
even if I know it doesn't want me
I carried that mango home
in my purse
like a second heart
I was ready to give away to you
but you never called
and Friday nights
inch away
when phones don't ring
I sliced the fruit
and ate it slowly
its juice snaking down
my wrist
this is how I eat my heart out
my fingers
sweet, sticky
the seed in my mouth
its coarse hairs
there's nothing left
I do not stop
wanting more
I do not know how

A Name That Isn't Mine

I know there is someone else
I would reproach

there isn't
*you would s*wear

but sometimes, late at night when I would wait for you,
she'd climb into my bones. I could feel her stillness in
my stomach. could taste her voice in my mouth. I tried
finding her on Facebook or Instagram. anything to give
her name a face. I wanted to know who was haunting
me. I wondered if I haunted her too. any woman you
mentioned became her. I began thinking of her more
often than I thought of you. she was a fever I couldn't
shake. until you'd come by and talk her out of my skin.
promised it was only me. I believed you. I chose to.

until tonight
when you said her name casually
when you thought I wasn't listening

and my bones
again

became hers

Rotting

I imagine you in her home. both of you at the dinner
table. studying. your legs close enough to touch. you, so
familiar to her. I imagine you sleeping beside her. her
breath a delicate hum over your skin. she's a friend. you
insist. *what am I*. we change the subject. her name glows
in the distance. I wonder how many other names I've yet
to see. how many more will come to find me. I don't ask. I
don't go looking for what I don't want to find.

Traditions

she told me
that a couple of weeks
before he died
he managed to walk
to her side of the bed
held her face
with his trembling fingers
and asked
we are happy, aren't we?

I thought of you then,
of the night
you pressed yourself into me
all frightened eyes and lips
asked if I had forgiven you

and I wanted to tell you
the everything of everything then

but instead,
like my mother to my father,
I nodded a tearful yes

Sacraments

I grew up Catholic
telling a man all my sins
waiting for forgiveness
and communion:
a man's flesh
again

it is no different
than the nights
I lay in your bed
confessing that
I can't forget
what I swore I would

you, sin and savior

my penance
God's name on my lips
as you make
a tabernacle
of me

Amherst

I am in a hotel room on the other side of the country. I am
laying in a bed where you and I have never touched. the
fireplace is beautiful. I ordered room service for breakfast.
the pancakes came with maple syrup. I thought of you
then. beneath this Massachusetts sky. the cold breathing
against the windows. I remembered the only morning I
spent in your home. sitting at your kitchen table, sharing a
stack of day-old pancakes you found in the fridge. I kissed
you goodbye hours later and still tasted the syrup. here, in
the present, I eat my meal alone. there is a flight waiting
to carry me home. I hadn't thought of you the entire trip.
until now. another city in which I have missed you. that
makes twelve of them this year. as if I carry you in my
luggage. unfolding you into every new bed. wearing you
on my long trip back to a place where we both live and I
still miss you.

How My First Tongue
Keeps You

there is a word in Spanish
that does not exist in English:

empalagar

to eat so much of something
you can't stand another bite

this is you and I

I am so sick
with the taste of you
I can't remember
savoring anyone else

The Ache

A Plot Twist

maybe I've been telling the story wrong

maybe you loved me so much
it feels like you didn't love me at all

Explanation

what happened?
the question
I've been spooning
into myself for weeks

there was the beginning,
your name a ripening fruit in my chest
the long hours of laughter and conversation
how easy it was to surrender
how quickly I turned you into my home

then came the conflict,
my fear, my lies
your drinking, your reproaches
my stubborn heart, yours,
the arguments
the nights
we didn't know
if we were
staying or leaving
all the men I tried to forget you with
how I'd return to my bed
angry that they weren't you

take me back, please

and you,
a sober man now
too sane to indulge
my drunken heart

couldn't

wouldn't

anymore

Last Straw

I can wait for you to:

finish school / take care of your health / focus on your
promotion / work on your sobriety / heal

I can't wait for you to:

decide I am worth loving

What You Taught Me

before you
I did not know that love could be
the knife, the hand, the wound,
the kiss that convinces you
there is no blood left to lose

Hangover

thirteen weeks since you loved me last / got one picture
of us in my phone / remember? / I do / I don't forget /
don't try to / I drink and I leave your name on the rim of
my glass / a deep red stain / I miss your voice / its rasp /
it was mine once / I thought / you don't drink / anymore /
sober boy / you stopped asking for a son / when you gave
up alcohol / I knew why / did I tell you the story of when
my father gave up drinking? / the year I turned eleven
/ I'd spent all summer in Gainesville, Georgia / when I
returned he was hardly home / AA meetings and soccer
games / kept him busy and clean / I missed him / I asked
God for things to change / stayed up all night waiting
for him / soon he was around more / so was the bottle /
so was his anger / I asked for that / I made it happen / I
understand why you're gone / I am not always a safe place
/ the daughter of an addict / my love must taste like a
hangover / of course you've stayed away / I wear enabler
and lover in the same skin / thirteen weeks / every Friday
night / this party girl whispers your name into her sheets /
I am a cup you can no longer drink from / I understand / I
wish I didn't

Nopales

my mother grows cactus in our garden. my father cut
the leaves from their homes. spent the afternoon slicing
the thorns off their bodies. leaving them smooth. new.
sometimes I would forget and sit at the table where he'd
been working. a thorn would end up on my finger or
my foot. Mami said that if left untouched, a thorn will
eventually make its way into your heart and kill you. I
believed her. I'd spend hours in the bathroom with a
tweezer. searching for the needle. I could feel it. it was
there. inching its way up my arm or leg.

this is you, isn't it?

years later
and I am not dead

I am hunched with a pen
searching for you

hoping to write you out

before you claim
the last parts of me

Hair

you'd complain
about my hair

how you always
found it in your sheets
after I'd gone home

I joked, back then,
that I was claiming
my territory

I wonder now
if anyone had ever found a curl
and been too afraid of the truth
to ask who it belonged to

like the day I was cooking dinner
and spotted a hair tie that wasn't mine
on your kitchen counter

all night, it was the loudest thing
in the apartment
a voice I wished I had never heard

Haunted

when someone you love
starts loving someone new
and that someone new
loves them back
you watch from a distance
hoping to see some of you
in their love

is this what it is to become a ghost?
is this how you haunt?
how you flicker the lights?
how you creak the floors?
how you wait for a body that is no longer yours?

Neon Nails

I keep these nails sharp

sometimes
when I'm making love
with someone new
I dig into their skin
just to see them flinch

the other day,
I heard you gave your new girl
my old pet name

I laughed

got my nails done again
searched for a new canvas
to claw them into

How To Miss What Doesn't Want To Be Missed

eat your fingers
one by one

the skin, the nerves,
the muscle,
the bones

you will be left
with hands
that can no longer
curl

into a question

that can no longer
ask

why not me?

After The Skin Infection, After The Hospital

the sick leg isn't a leg. it is you.
I am not myself. I am four years of waiting.
the illness turns the leg
into a feverish limb
it is the universe or god or
my own anatomy
begging me to leave you behind.
I wait. I am four years of waiting.
I am home now and my leg is my leg again.
all scarred, bandaged, full of pus. I can hardly walk.

you never called.

Loophole

there is a trick I learned long ago:

love a man that won't love you back
and you'll always be free

what is freedom but the absence of everything?

everything including
you

Clean and Fed

I thought that if I cleaned enough of your apartment, I'd
scrub the other women out. isn't that how it is done? keep
you clean, fed and fucked and you won't wander? I must
have read my manual wrong because I began wanting
things and your apartment wasn't big enough for all my
want. I first noticed the hunger growing behind my eyes.
then it took root beneath my tongue. then every time I
touched you it got in the way. one morning, I woke and
it was all that I was. I couldn't keep loving you. not like
that. not in parts. not in shifts. not in favors. not as a
reward. so I left. how beautiful that's been. how rested my
hands have become. how free I am now that I've stopped
working for your love.

Terrible

the last fight came after I was hospitalized

you talked and talked and talked and talked and talked
and talked and talked about how awful I am / how I did
you wrong / how I fucked other men / how I didn't lend
you money / how I lied / how you hate me / how selfish I
am / how now I want to be who I never was / how I don't
love you / how I don't know what love is / how I give
everyone what I am supposed to keep for you / how I am
terrible / how I don't know how hard it's been dealing
with me / this monster / this headache / this bitch that is
incapable of loving you how you want to be loved

I listened. I sobbed.
I was a river again

through the dark the last words found me
five small snakes slowly
winding themselves into my mouth:

get out of my life.

Los Corvos

we keep a machete in our home
Mami uses it to cut the weeds
on Saturday afternoons
you'll find her in our garden
on her hands and knees
swinging away

Mamita, mami's mami,
used to grab her own machete
back in El Salvador
and head down to the river
she'd cut away at tree branches
and overgrown bamboo
her tiny frame in the distance
her right arm extended
the blade catching the sunlight

I come from women
who fend for themselves

the blade is our friend

and you?

you are a weed

I know how to slice you out of me

The Burning

I remember the third night we spent together
I was on my knees with a mouthful of you
when you asked,
if I would be willing to do this for other men
if I would let you charge them for my pretty little mouth

I did not say a word
I did not pull you out of me
I closed my eyes
I held my breath
I swallowed you when you came
we never spoke of it again

the fifth night
you asked if you could
put on some porn
while we made love
I said I didn't mind
but I watched your face
as you stared at the screen
you never looked at me that way
you didn't look at me at all
I began numbering the times you called me beautiful
I hardly had anything to count

on the eleventh night
you asked if I could come keep your loneliness at bay
we sat on opposite ends of your couch
we didn't speak for hours
I leaned over and ran my finger down your shoulder
you shrugged me off while texting someone else
I got up, walked to the bathroom, closed the door
ran the water while I sobbed
when I returned,
you mentioned you needed money

I offered to give you anything you'd like
just to turn you human again

you kissed me
softly
slowly
and I held my breath
for days

then came the flood
the part where I forgot I do not know how to swim
how to dive into a man and come back up for air
the nights
I sawed off my hands
and left them on your lap
the nights
I unhinged my jaw
swallowed my feet
turned myself inside out
the nights
you called me lazy,
whispered *clingy*

I forgave it all
because you were beautiful on the good days
because you kissed me and
I became steam seeping through the floorboards
because in the dark
I own you now.
you are mine.
sounds a lot like
I love you

I made up excuses to stay
refused to give you up
I knew I wasn't supposed to be
anything but grateful
it was our agreement
when I tried to buy your love
with my wallet and my mouth

but when I'd had enough
threatened to leave
you said I had become too complicated
I had stopped being fun
that someone would be happy to take my place
that you had been nothing but a perfect gentleman
and if I needed to write a poem to get over it , I could

and that's when
I understood
why some women
light shit on fire

it isn't about
getting you to come back
it is realizing that
who I was when I let you stay
needed to be burned to the ground

like that third night we spent together
when I was on my knees
with a mouthful of you

I should have bit down

I should have turned
this pretty little mouth
into a blowtorch

I should have
left you in a pile of ash

a reminder
of who I can become
if I don't leave
when I see smoke
disguised
as a
man

The
Return

Corazón Heals Herself

and so, you loved him
for a long, long time
so long
you thought you couldn't stop

and he didn't love you back
didn't beg you to stay
kept on living without you

you are still alive
still laugh with your own mouth
still point at the moon with the same finger

you loved him
because you're so good at loving
so good at asking *what can I give you?*
what do you need?

remember the time you thought you were dying and you asked yourself to stay? remember when you hated your own body and asked yourself to stop? remember when you held your dead father's hand and refused to call him gone? remember the time a man sunk his teeth into your breasts and you managed to run? remember the times you walked away from hurt? the times you said *no?* said *me first?* called yourself beautiful and believed it. called yourself home and became it. turned yourself into a song. full volume. your sweet face leaned into a mirror. your full lips painted red. your dark curls, a halo. your skin, spun gold. you, your greatest love. the salve for all wounds.

yes, he didn't love you

you are still alive
still pointing at the moon
with all of your fingers
extended
towards
your reflection

Bruja

I used to think
of myself as lonely,
as a hungry bruja
howling at the moon
for a body to hold
but ever since the last man left
-    The one who called
      himself animal
      and I didn't correct
I've been casting spells
for new things:
poems
good hair days
a pot of coffee
a delicious book to read
something new to laugh at
a stage for my witchcraft
full moons to land on my empty bed
a howl, so clear, that
I become enough body to hold
for my restless arms

When You Both Love Men That Don't Deserve Your Love

for Angela

she lets out a long sigh
both hands on the steering wheel

the highway winds
before us
we've both just finished
saying the names of men
that take up too
much space
in the car

we turn the radio up high
our song is on
we sing it loud

ain't no room
for heartache
now

in the rearview mirror
we catch a glimpse
of what could have been
but, thank god,
isn't

Celebration

tonight, I'm gonna dance like the sky ain't falling
like my bones don't rattle for someone else
like I don't gotta peel myself out of bed
like it didn't take two hours of holding my own hand
just to walk out the door

tonight
I'll dance
I'll be alive

and ain't that worth the party?

Fly Girl

I was 22 and a hot air balloon
never really here
just over - there
I watched women who danced
and said
that isn't me
I
can't
move

I was 24 and mirror in a closet
somewhere to look
then leave
I let my eyes eat
music videos
and said
never
me

I was 30 and awake
four shots of Patrón
the DJ played my favorite song
and I was the dance floor
I was the bodies and bass
I was the strobe lights
look at how I laughed
this was me
free
my hair frizzed with sweat
glasses fogged
my hips gyrating like
I didn't teach them

33 and I am a party girl

and why not?

everything else
is a cage

this body is fly
when it touches ground

watch

Gorda

you take the word. the one that sliced through you like a
knife through pan fresco. the one your Tío called you de
cariño. the one the boys in school hissed as you walked
by. you take the word and write it down. one time. two
times. say it in English. Fat. it hurts that way too. maybe
even more. the word now is a blade. two sides. you write
it down. hundreds of times. you start saying it to describe
yourself. you don't flinch. others do. they fear it more
than they do Bitch or Whore. the word gives you power.
you date a few men. they won't say the word. they prefer
thick or *curvy* or *big*. you say you want to hear it. like
you hear your name. some can't say it without laughing.
embarrassed. like you just flashed a nipple in public. they
call you brave. you say it's just the parts of you that you
can touch. like short. like glasses. like curly. like brown.
the word is home. you write it down. you write it down.
you write it down. you are a bruja when you write it down.
look at that magic, Gorda. mira que bella. Gorda. your
body answers: *hello. I'm here. thank you.*

Wild

the boys always find you
grind their pelvises against you for a handful of songs
their mouths search for your mouth in the dark
your lipstick smears across their smile
you leave together
and both your bodies end up naked on some bed

you write about these conquests
the power to live like a man
to spit on the same floor you stand on
to scratch any itch you have

your family is scandalized by you
thirty-three and single
no children
no house to cook and clean in
no one to serve after your mother dies

all you have is the years
that are piling around you like dust
soon your heart
will be the last one at the station

aren't you scared the train is gonna leave you?
your uncle asks

ay Tío, that train came and went and I jumped off!

you both laugh at the wild woman you've become

On Laughter

sometimes I laugh so hard the world spins. I laugh with
all of my body. the arms. the toes. the back of knees. the
place where elbows fold. the lumpy shoulders. the belly
like a sack of crumpled clothes. the tonsils. the hip bone.
it all explodes all at once. I can't breathe then. (the lungs
are busy laughing too). my eyes spill a few drops of sky
and I shake and shake and shake. I like myself best when
I am laughing. bursting. all of me. the best of me.

Sisterhood

homegirl on the bus asks
if I have a bobby pin

I pull one out from between my curls
hand it to her

she in turn,
parts her hair
slicks back a strand
pins it down

we nod
and continue
making our way
through Los Angeles
late at night

The House on Parkman Avenue

my five-month-old nephew laughs. a brand-new baby
laugh. his little face full of joy. my niece climbs onto my
lap. she talks a mile a minute. a story about an invented
bunny we've named Fluffy. in the next room Mami is
on the phone with my Tío who lives back home. she's
shouting. it's her long distance voice. my youngest sister
chuckles at her computer. my other sister, the mother, is
in the kitchen. the babies, their toys, bottles and I crowd
the couch. in two days I fly out to another city, I tell this to
my niece. *What are you gonna do there?* she asks. *I'm gonna
tell them stories about us and how much I love you*, I kiss into
her dark hair. she nods. the baby laughs again.

Mami

Cosas que de niña mi Mami me enseñó:

el corazón se estira millas y millas
el amor vive en dos países al mismo tiempo
el cariño nunca olvida
la comida es como uno viaja más rápido
una canción es eterna
la muerte no nos quita lo nuestro
mi familia es Dios vivo
y mi madre
es toda la salvación que necesito

Compilation

all my poems are about love
all my poems are about some boy
all my poems are about my fat
all my poems are about my parents
all my poems are about my Spanish
my El Salvador
my English
my Los Angeles
my pre-gentrification Silverlake
my Echo Park before food trucks and yoga parties
my belly swinging by vegan restaurants
my double chin laughing in overpriced coffee shops
my minimum wage paycheck
my staying too long in too many places
my poor choice in men
my online dating
my hope
my bad dates
my ex boyfriends
my ex boyfriends and their girlfriends
my niece
my niece and her laughter
my niece and her questions
my niece and her hands pressed against my face
her hands wet with the tears on my face
my depression
my secret sadness
my ocean always asking for my body
my anxiety whispering my name at the nape of my neck
my hands, how they listened
and slammed against my body
my body
my body and how no one ever saw the bruises
because no one ever saw my body
all my poems are about my body
my brown girl body
my 'everyone has an opinion about this body' body

my 'I have to fight to love it every fucking day' body
my big fat beautiful body
my smile
my red lipstick smile
my curly Salvadoran hair
my mami's hair in my hair
my Mami
my Papi
my drunk and angry Papi
my Papi yelling out my name in the middle of the night
my Papi and his belt against my skin
my Papi's belt and how it whistled in the air before
finding me
my long nights counting his snores
my burying him ten years before he died
my watching him die
my exhale when he died
my life after he died
my good life after he died
my happiness in his absence
my guilt
my love
my heart
my daddy
all my poems are about my parents
my immigrant parents
my hardworking parents
my hardly any English parents
my Saturday afternoon listening to Juan Gabriel parents
my early Sunday morning mass parents
my sisters and I in our prettiest dresses
my sisters
my first friends
my first saviors
my first lesson in getting the fuck over it
my loud ass sisters

83

my singing until Mami yells 'shut the hell up, this isn't a
musical' sisters
my there's been an earthquake better check on Yesika
sisters
my no one gets it like you do sisters
all of my poems are about love
the times it came in floods
the years I forgot what it was
all my poems are collection plates
I fill
and fill
and fill
and fill
and
fill
I have yet to come up empty
I don't think I ever will
thank God for my poems
for how they always find me
for my hands who receive them
for my heart
who always believes them

The End

what a joy, this book. the weeks I spent clawing at
my heart for it. the years I spent writing as if my life
depended on it (it did). Corazón began a long time before
I decided to write a book. before any of the men I have
loved. before the relationships ended and became poems.
here are the people from the before. the during. the
survival. without them I would not be who I am.
Gracias.

Not a Cult

Daniel Lisi, we sat in the Cafe Tropical and you asked
if I wanted to publish a book. I said yes. you made
accomplishing a lifelong goal as easy as ordering a cafe
con leche. **Cassidy Trier**, you read my poems and you
saw my heart. my goodness this book cover you
designed. it is as if you knew everything there is to know
about my love. **Sa ia Elhillo**, thank you for untangling
my words, your gentle input has been the polish this
book needed. the rest of the team, thank you for
midwifing my biggest dream.
The staff at **Cafe Tropical**, now that Silverlake is
gentrified, your establishment is one of the last places
that feels like home. I wrote this manuscript during a
heatwave, sobbing my eyes out at your corner table, god
bless your air conditioning.
Zoe Muñoz, you kept me company during the two weeks
of coffee, empanadas and combing through poems. you
were the raft that brought me and this book ashore.
Da Poetry Lounge
Poetri, Gimel, Dante, Edwin, Jasmine, Fisseha, Katrina,
Vanessa, Bird, Donny, Carolyn, Danielle, Maceo, Carrie,
Alyesha, Cuban, Terisa, Aman, Kito, Angelena, Saint and
so so so many other names I am scared to forget. You are
my family, my classroom and my church. I am who I am
because of you and all the ways I discovered love through
you.
Joel Jaimes, you've helped me bring my poems to the

world for years. you translate life for me when I don't get it. te quiero mucho.

Javon Johnson, when I have needed the truth I have found it in you. thank you for always challenging me to show up.

Shihan Van Clief, thank you for being the constant reminder that my story is so much more than I think it is.

Angela Aguirre, we have cried all the tears there are to cry and danced all the songs there are to dance together. thank you for loving me, for Chingona Fire, for being exactly what I've needed and didn't know to ask for.

Mi Familia, those I was raised with. los que quedan en El Salvador. I am constantly trying to tell our stories. I inherited this precocious heart from you. you are my greatest treasure.

Jackie, the pool in the hollywood hills. access to your quiet apartment. you give me a safe space to sort through all the feelings before writing them down. I love you, cousin.

Jennifer and Julissa, my sisters, my life. thank you for letting me tell the world all about our home and family. for the space you've given my art. the patience you've given me.

Saya and Henry, you have made a Tia and better woman out of me.

Papi, you are in every poem I write. in every room I perform in. in every day I live.

Mami este es el fruto de su amor. de su paciencia. sin usted yo soy nada. por usted yo soy todo.

You. dear reader. thank you. thank you. thank you. for seeing me. for believing in me. for loving me. for giving me all I never thought I'd deserve. may my heart always reflect yours. may I continue being worthy of you, mi corazón.

About the Author

Yesika Salgado is a Los Angeles based Salvadoran poet who writes about her family, her culture, her city, and her brown body. She has shared her work in venues and campuses throughout the country. Salgado is a four time member of Da Poetry Lounge Slam Team and a 2017 and 2018 National Poetry Slam finalist. Her work has been featured in *The Los Angeles Times, Latina Magazine, Univision, Vibe Magazine, Huffington Post, NPR, TEDx* and many digital platforms. She is the co-founder of the Latina feminist collective Chingona Fire and an internationally recognized body positivity activist. Yesika is the author of the Amazon best-sellers *Corazón* and *Tesoro*, published with Not a Cult.